*your dog*

# A LIFETIME
# RECORD

**EUKANUBA**

**An informative and entertaining activity book for dog lovers.**

*This is an activity book. Although it is full of useful information and practical tips, it is not just for reading: this book wants to be used!*

*Record all those precious moments and add your favorite pictures. Make notes about your dog's growth, health and training. Fill in questions and charts and check his nutritional needs. Your dog is like no other. So he certainly deserves a book that's like no other book. Enjoy your dog, enjoy completing his own book.*

*let's begin*

# AT THE
# BEGINNING

| | |
|---|---|
| 1 | Full name: |
| 2 | Pet name: |
| 3 | Sex: |
| 4 | Date of birth: |
| 5 | Place of birth: |
| 6 | Color (eyes and coat): |
| 7 | Distinguishing Markings: |
| 8 | Vaccinations: |

☎ Telephone number of veterinarian:

☎ Telephone number of pet insurance company:

*Outline your dog's paw in here.*

Keep this data at hand, for whenever you need to call the vet.

### Medical record

| Vaccinations | 1* | 2* | 3* | 4* | 5* |
|---|---|---|---|---|---|
| Date | | | | | |
| Illnesses | date | type | | | |
| | | | | | |
| | | | | | |
| Treatment | date | type | | | |
| | | | | | |
| | | | | | |

1* : Canine Distemper / Hepatitis / Leptospirosis
2* : Canine Parvovirus
3* : Coronavirus
4* : Bordatella / Influenza
5* : Rabies

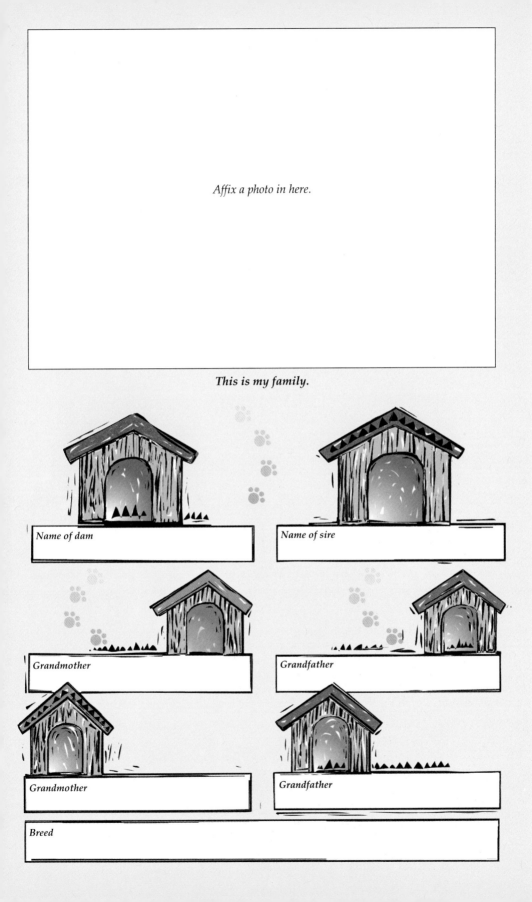

*Affix a photo in here.*

**This is my family.**

Name of dam

Name of sire

Grandmother

Grandfather

Grandmother

Grandfather

Breed

# the start of
# A NEW
# LIFE

**e start of a new life.**
nen you bring a puppy into
ur home for the first time,
ll probably feel frightened
d apprehensive. After all, he
n a strange new environment.
u may comfort him by
lding him as shown, with
e hand under his chest and
e other supporting his hind

gs. By holding him in this
ay, he will feel secure and
otected.

**s own place.**
ur puppy needs a place of
s own. Give him a box or a
g bed inside a pen - in a
arm, draught-free corner.
itting a box on its side to
ake an enclosed bed will
ake him feel even more
cure. Why? Well, a cave was
me to the dog's wolf-like
cestor, so your puppy
stinctively feels cosy and safe
anything remotely
sembling a cave, even if its
st a turned-over box. Add
me warm, washable bedding
ke a blanket or towel) and

your puppy's place is complete.

**Naming your puppy.**
Remember, when choosing a
name for your puppy, two-
syllable names that end in a
vowel, like Tasha or Bonzo, are
easiest for a dog to recall.

**From bowls to brushes.**
Eating and drinking bowls,
preferably made from stainless
steel, crockery or glass, should
be placed in a quiet, out-of-the-
way place. They should not be
easy to tip-over and plenty of
fresh water should be available
at all times. To complete your
dog's outfit, he should have a
collar and lead with dog tag
(detailing name, address
and/or phone number), plus a
comb and brush for grooming.

**TIPS TIPS TIPS TIPS TIPS TIPS TIPS**

Never send your dog to his
bed because you are angry.
He'll associate this place with
punishment, and develop a
dislike of it.

Instinctively a puppy may
want to defend his food and
may even try to bite you.
Correct him, show him you
are the boss and gradually
he will come to accept this.

For larger puppies and for
older dogs, a stand under
their eating bowls is
preferable. Don't forget the
drinking bowl, too!

*Dear diary, my first day in my new home:*

### House-training: don't worry.

Many people fear that house-training a puppy is troublesome. True, it takes attention, patience and perseverance. Some dogs are more trainable than others; however, it does not have to be difficult and it does not have to take a long time - as long as you stick to a few basic principles.

### Elementary schooling.

Begin house-training your puppy right away.

Start by putting him on a regular feeding schedule and make frequent trips outside. The signs to look for are: your puppy walking around in

Never, ever rub your dog's nose in his own mess. He won't understand what you are doing to him and he will learn nothing from it.

To clean up his mess, do not use ammonia-based cleaners, because chemically these resemble urine. Once cleaned, block off the area until it's dry. Otherwise, your pup will be back to investigate the smell and may feel the urge to repeat the mess.

Using a box with high sides at night may be helpful. A puppy that sleeps in an enclosed area has no urge to wander around to relieve himself elsewhere in the house.

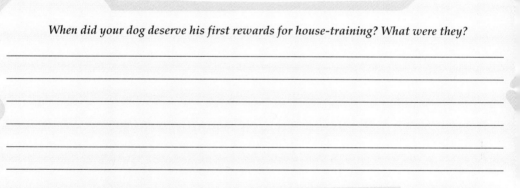

*When did your dog deserve his first rewards for house-training? What were they?*

_____

_____

_____

_____

_____

_____

circles, sitting or whining at the door, or your puppy voluntarily giving you "the look". When you catch him in the act, immediately take him outside to finish. When he has finished relieving himself, quietly praise him and bring him back inside. Soon he will connect "going" outdoors with praise.

### Timing is the word.

The best times to take your puppy outside are first thing in the morning, just after his naps, upon returning home to

a puppy that has been left alone, just after meals and last thing in the evening.

Accidents do happen. Should you discover a mess, do not raise your voice or smack your pup. While he'll certainly cower in fear, he's too young to connect your reprimand with his mess.

Although of course, every dog has its own character and development pattern - as a rule of thumb, a three-month old puppy can be house-trained within two weeks, but a lot depends on the owner's patience and common sense.

Affix a photo in here.

See me growing from this cute, little puppy . . . .

Affix a photo in here.

. . . . . . to the irresistibly handsome dog I am now.

## The serious business of playing.

Puppies love playing and definitely need to play.
To them, it's not a game, it's an indispensable part of growing up. In playing, puppies train their stalking and chasing abilities and their capacities for guarding and hunting.
So it's a game, but at the same

## Helping him teethe.

Puppies teethe between the ages of three and six months, and they need to chew on something to help the new teeth come through.
Help avoid accidents by giving your puppy a choice of good, indestructible objects to chew. Your pet shop will have an excellent selection.

Don't give your puppy real bones, not even to play with. These could splinter, hurt his mouth and cause choking if a sliver is swallowed.

Do not give a puppy an old shoe, or any shoe-like material to chew. Many people do, and this will make him think all shoes are acceptable for chewing. Moreover, some shoes contain potentially poisonous tanning agents.

time it's serious business, too. Remember, even when your dog has grown up, he still needs you to spend a lot of time playing with him.

Watch out for choking or swallowing and make sure his toys are not too small.
Make his toy especially attractive to him by playing games with it.

Help your puppy avoid the wrong things by keeping them away from him. Especially make sure that cleansers, paint thinners, household chemicals and other harmful substances are safely out of his reach.

*Affix a photo in here.*

*It may be a game, but I'm very serious about it!*

**Choice of toys.**

Give your puppy his favorite toy whenever he starts to chew an unacceptable object. Say "No" sternly, take the forbidden item away and replace it with a rubber ball or bone. When he starts to chew on his own toy, praise him for good behavior. He'll respond happily. Not all toys are equally suitable for puppies. Rubber is suitable only when it is really solid and hard. Hide chews may be a good choice, but make sure they cannot be torn, even after prolonged chewing. Objects from which pieces can be torn should be avoided at all times.

*I love it! These are my favorite toys:*

# FOOD FOR THOUGHT

# Food for thought.

Everyone has heard about vitamins and minerals, carbohydrates and fiber, fats and proteins, but few people know the full importance of these nutrients. These pages are about food and growth, and your dog's digestive system. You'll find lots of feeding tips for healthy growth. But let's start at the very beginning.

Feeding your dog table scraps is not advisable as it provides an incomplete and unbalanced diet.

So what does your dog really need for a fully balanced diet? To understand your dog's nutritional needs, test your knowledge below.

## Fats for energy.

The body's primary need is energy. Energy to maintain the body, to breathe, to run, to play and to grow. Fat is the best source of this energy. In fact, fats are a small miracle in themselves. They contain about 2.5 times more available energy than proteins or carbohydrates. Fats are essential in every dog's diet.

Fats provide and promote the assimilation of fat-soluble vitamins (A,D,E and K), protect against cold, provide protection for vulnerable organs, give a healthy coat and enhance the taste of food.

## No doubt about it: he's a carnivore.

Your dog is a descendant of a large family of carnivores: wild, predatory animals surviving by eating other animals. His digestive system is very similar to that of his forefather's. This means your dog is a meat-eater, but not an animal that eats meat exclusively, although he is best fed with protein and fat from meat sources, rather than from cheaper vegetable substitutes.

## Test your knowledge:

1. **Which fats are best for your dog?**
   a. *vegetable fats*
   b. *animal-based fats*
   c. *synthetic fats*

2. **Which option provides the best source(s) of protein for your dog?**
   a. *chicken and eggs*
   b. *soy*
   c. *wheat*

*The right answers to the questions are 1.b and 2.a.*

### Building the body with proteins.

Proteins are the building blocks for muscle, bone, blood and other tissues, as well as for the immune system which helps prevent disease. They are also vital for the hormones and enzymes that keep the cellular factories going.

Proteins can be found in meat, fish, soya or wheat middlings, as well as in chicken and egg. The proteins in the latter two are highly digestible and result in small, firm stools.

### Carbohydrates and fiber.

For short-term energy, ie: running and jumping,

### Vitamins and minerals.

Vitamins and minerals help your dog develop his bones, teeth and coat and they protect him from disease and infection. No breed requires more or less vitamins and minerals than another. What matters is the actual daily intake. A complete and balanced food should contain all the required vitamins, minerals and trace elements, balanced to the energy content of the food. An excess of specific vitamins may even lead to problems, like skeletal diseases. Often, more health problems are created by oversupply of vitamins and minerals than by deficiencies.

### Last but not least, water.

On a volume basis, water is the most important nutrient. Your dog should have an ample supply of fresh, clean water available at all times - even a small percentage loss of body water may cause your dog distress - a 15% loss of body water can be fatal.

Proteins can be broken down into amino acids. Some of these are manufactured by the body. Others, however, are termed essential amino acids, because they must be present in the daily diet. For your dog to remain healthy, his diet must contain adequate amounts of each of 10 essential amino acids in order to provide the required building blocks for growth and tissue repair.

carbohydrates are the primary source. Carbohydrates also provide fiber. Crude fiber is by definition not digestible, its function is purely mechanical. Total dietary fiber is responsible for optimal intestinal health and transit time. In other words, it functions as a bowel regulator and influences the absorption of nutrients, including water from the gut.

bored with their food.
The need for variety is a human trait. Eukanuba Dog Foods are complete and balanced and contain a variety of nutritious ingredients. However, if you want to vary your dog's diet, you can mix a complete dry food with a complete canned food.

The Iams Company offers several varieties of Iams canned food that will compliment the dry diet of Eukanuba.
Never feed him your favorite foods as a replacement for his meals or as a reward.
Use dog biscuits if you want to reward him.

*Affix a photo in here.*

## eding your puppy.

puppy can grow as much in first year as a human being es in the first fourteen years. your dog's nutritional quirements may never be ore demanding than when 's a young puppy. It takes a reful balance of high-quality gredients to provide these quirements. Eukanuba ppy Small or Large Bite and kanuba Lamb & Rice For ppies are specially rmulated for the first months your dog's life.
e special size and texture of e food have been created to ake it easier for your puppy eat. As it is so digestible, he ll utilize more of the food he kes in for nourishment than th many other foods. This eans optimum health and all, firm stools for easy an up.

## ogs don't need variety.
ntrary to popular belief, gs do not get tired of or

*Rewarding my friend.*

### TIPS TIPS TIPS TIPS TIPS TIPS TIPS TIPS TIPS TIPS TIPS TIPS TIPS TIPS TIPS

Growing puppies have tremendous energy requirements, yet have a very small stomach capacity. Therefore, rather than feed a canned food, it is better to feed them a top quality, complete, dry food.

Most dogs can switch from any Eukanuba puppy food at the age of 12 - 18 months to any Eukanuba adult product. Eukanuba Adult Maintenance, Eukanuba The Original Premium, Eukanuba Light or Eukanuba Lamb & Rice For Dogs depending on the dog's preference.

## How much and when?

For a small or medium breed puppy, scheduled portion controlled feeding is recommended. This means you feed your puppy his daily ration at specified times throughout the day. For the first six months, feed 1/3 in the morning, 1/3 in the afternoon and 1/3 in the evening. After six months of age, switch to 1/2 in the morning and 1/2 in the evening.

For large or giant breeds, a portion controlled method is strongly recommended.

Alternatively, you can put your puppy's daily portion in his bowl in the morning and allow him to eat it throughout the day as his body requires nourishment.

Remember, gradual growth is essential and it is important to keep your puppy lean. Puppies that grow too fast may develop bone-defects.

*In this diagram you see growth curves for several breeds and t of a child. As you can see, some breeds continue to grow long than others. A child keeps on growing much longer. Put down a dot every month at the appropriate weight for yo own dog, and connect the dots. You'll have your own dog's growth curve.*

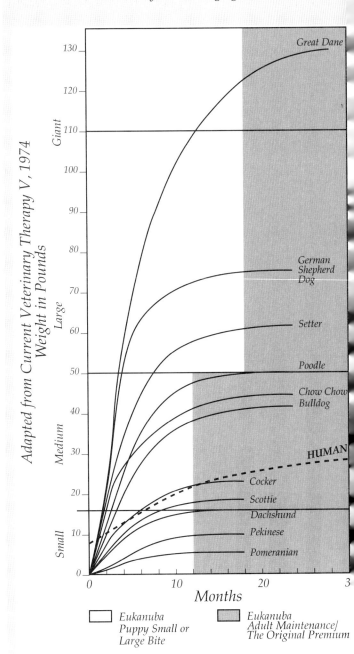

* Depending on the dog's activity and preference

# Guide to adult dogs body weight (in Lbs).

| Breed | Male | Female | Breed | Male | Female | Breed | Male | Female |
|---|---|---|---|---|---|---|---|---|
| ffenpinscher | 7 - 8 | 7 - 8 | Dalmatian | 50 - 65 | 45 - 55 | Pug | 14 - 18 | 14 - 18 |
| fghan Hound | - 60 | - 50 | Doberman | 65 - 80 | 55 - 70 | Rottweiler | 90 - 110 | 80 - 100 |
| iredale Terrier | 45 - 60 | 40 - 55 | English Setter | 60 - 75 | 55 - 65 | Rhodesian | | |
| kita | 75 - 110 | 70 - 100 | Fox Terrier | 17 - 19 | 15 - 17 | Ridgeback | - 75 | - 65 |
| laskan Malemute | 85 - 95 | 75 - 85 | French Bulldog | 20 - 28 | 20 - 28 | St. Bernard | 130 - 180 | 120 - 160 |
| asenji | - 24 | - 22 | German | | | Saluki | 50 - 70 | 45 - 65 |
| asset Hound | 65 - 75 | 50 - 65 | Shepherd Dog | 75 - 90 | 65 - 80 | Samoyed | 50 - 65 | 45 - 60 |
| eagle | 13 - 18 | 13 - 16 | Golden Retriever | 65 - 75 | 55 - 65 | Schnauzer, | | |
| earded Collie | 55 - 65 | 50 - 60 | Great Dane | 120 - 180 | 100 - 130 | minature | 16 - 18 | 12 - 16 |
| edlington Terrier | 17 - 23 | 17 - 23 | Greyhound | 65 - 75 | 60 - 65 | Schnauzer, | | |
| elgian Sheep Dog | 60 - 70 | 43 - 55 | Irish Setter | - 70 | - 60 | standard | 30 - 40 | 25 - 35 |
| ernese | | | Irish Terrier | - 27 | - 25 | Schnauzer, giant | 70 - 85 | 60 - 75 |
| Mountain Dog | 75 - 90 | 65 - 80 | Irish Wolfhound | 120 - 180 | 105 - 150 | Scottish | | |
| ichon Frise | 9 - 12 | 9 - 12 | Keeshonden | 40 - 50 | 40 - 50 | Deerhound | 85 - 110 | 75 - 95 |
| loodhound | 90 - 110 | 80 - 100 | Kerry Blue Terrier | 33 - 40 | 30 - 38 | Scottish Terrier | 19 - 22 | 18 - 21 |
| order Collie | 60 - 75 | 55 - 65 | Labrador Retriever | 65 - 80 | 55 - 70 | Shar Pei | 45 - 55 | 35 - 45 |
| order Terrier | 13 - 15.5 | 11.5 - 14 | Lakeland Terrier | - 17 | - 17 | Shetland Sheepdog | 16 - 22 | 14 - 18 |
| orzoi | 75 - 105 | 70 - 90 | Lhasa Apso | 13 - 15 | 13 - 15 | Shih Tzu | 12 - 17 | 10 - 15 |
| ouvier | | | Maltese | 4 - 6 | 4 - 6 | Siberian Husky | 45 - 60 | 35 - 50 |
| des Flandres | 65 - 75 | 60 - 70 | Mastiff | 175 - 190 | 160 - 180 | Spaniel, English | | |
| oxer | 55 - 70 | 50 - 60 | Newfoundland | 130 - 150 | 100 - 120 | Springer | 49 - 55 | 40 - 45 |
| riard | 65 - 75 | 60 - 70 | Norfolk Terrier | 11 - 12 | 11 - 12 | Staffordshire Bull | | |
| ulldog | 45 - 55 | 40 - 50 | Norwich Terrier | 11 - 12 | 11 - 12 | Terrier | 28 - 38 | 24 - 34 |
| ullmastiff | 110 - 130 | 100 - 120 | Old English | | | Tibetan Spaniel | 9 - 15 | 9 - 15 |
| ull Terrier | 52 - 62 | 45 - 55 | Sheepdog | 60 - 70 | 60 - 70 | Tibetan Terrier | 18 - 30 | 18 - 30 |
| airn Terrier | - 14 | - 13 | Papillon | 8 - 10 | 7 - 9 | Weimaraner | 60 - 75 | 55 - 70 |
| hihuahua | 2.5 - 7.5 | 2.5 - 7.5 | Pekingese | 10 - 14 | 10 - 14 | West Highland | | |
| how Chow | 45 - 60 | 40 - 50 | Pointer | 55 - 75 | 45 - 64 | White Terrier | 12 - 14 | 11 - 13 |
| ocker Spaniel | 25 - 30 | 20 - 25 | Pomeranian | 4 - 7 | 3 - 5 | Welsh Corgi | 30 - 38 | 25 - 34 |
| achshund, | | | Poodle, standard | 50 - 60 | 45 - 55 | Whippet | 20 - 28 | 18 - 23 |
| standard | 16 - 22 | 16 - 22 | Poodle, miniature | 17 - 20 | 15 - 20 | Yorkshire Terrier | 4 - 6 | 3 - 6 |

## Weighing your dog (and yourself).

To weigh your dog, stand on the scale yourself and note your own weight. Now take your dog in your arms and weigh again. Subtract your own weight from the combined weight.
The remainder is your dog's weight.

## Checking for obesity.

THIN. Ribs and pelvic bones obviously apparent. Easily visible waist and abdominal tuck.

IDEAL. Ribs palpable without excess fat covering. Waist observed behind ribs when viewed from above. Abdomen tucked up when viewed from the side.

OBESE. Ribs not easily palpable under a heavy fat covering. Fat deposits noticeable at the back and at the base of tail. Waist barely visible or absent. No abdominal tuck, may even exhibit obvious abdominal distension.

## *Feeding Eukanuba.*
### *How much and how often should you feed your dog?*

**EUKANUBA PUPPY SMALL OR LARGE BITES**

| Puppy's Weight (in lbs.) | Suggested feeding amount | | | |
|---|---|---|---|---|
| | 6-11 Weeks | 3-4 Months | 5-7 Months | 8-12 Months |
| | Cups per Day* | | | |
| 3 - 5 | $^3/_4$ - $1^1/_3$ | $^3/_4$ - $1^1/_4$ | $^1/_2$ - $^3/_4$ | $^1/_3$ - $^2/_3$ |
| 5 - 10 | $1^1/_3$ - $2^1/_4$ | $1^1/_4$ - 2 | $^3/_4$ - $1^1/_4$ | $^2/_3$ - 1 |
| 10 - 20 | $2^1/_4$ - $3^1/_3$ | 2 - $3^1/_4$ | $1^1/_4$ - 2 | 1 - $1^2/_3$ |
| 20 - 30 | $3^1/_3$ - $4^1/_2$ | $3^1/_4$ - $4^1/_4$ | 2 - $2^2/_3$ | $1^2/_3$ - $2^1/_4$ |
| 30 - 40 | $4^1/_2$ - $5^1/_3$ | $4^1/_4$ - 5 | $2^2/_3$ - $3^1/_4$ | $2^1/_4$ - $2^2/_3$ |
| 40 - 60 | | 5 - $6^2/_3$ | $3^1/_4$ - $4^1/_2$ | $2^2/_3$ - $3^1/_2$ |
| 60 - 80 | | $6^2/_3$ - 8 | $4^1/_2$ - $5^1/_4$ | $3^1/_2$ - $4^1/_4$ |
| 80 -100 | | | $5^1/_4$ - 6 | $4^1/_4$ - 5 |

*Portions are based on a standard 8-oz measuring cup.

**EUKANUBA ☙: PUPPY**

**EUKANUBA NATURAL LAMB & RICE FORMULA FOR PUPPIES**

| Puppy's Weight (in lbs.) | Suggested feeding amount | | | |
|---|---|---|---|---|
| | 6-11 Weeks | 3-4 Months | 5-7 Months | 8-12 Months |
| | Cups per Day* | | | |
| 3 - 5 | 1 - $1^2/_3$ | 1 - $1^1/_2$ | $^2/_3$ -1 | $^1/_2$ - $^3/_4$ |
| 5 - 10 | $1^2/_3$ - $2^1/_2$ | $1^1/_2$ - $2^1/_2$ | 1 - $1^1/_2$ | $^3/_4$ - $1^1/_4$ |
| 10 - 20 | $2^1/_2$ - 4 | $2^1/_2$ - $3^3/_4$ | $1^1/_2$ - $2^1/_2$ | $1^1/_4$ - 2 |
| 20 - 30 | 4 - $5^1/_3$ | $3^3/_4$ - 5 | $2^1/_2$ - $3^1/_4$ | 2 - $2^2/_3$ |
| 30 - 40 | $5^1/_3$ - $6^1/_2$ | 5 - 6 | $3^1/_4$ - 4 | $2^2/_3$ - $3^1/_4$ |
| 40 - 60 | | 6 - 8 | 4 - 5 | $3^1/_4$ - $4^1/_4$ |
| 60 - 80 | | 8 - $9^3/_4$ | 5 - $6^1/_4$ | $4^1/_4$ - 5 |
| 80 -100 | | | $6^1/_4$ - $7^1/_4$ | 5 - 6 |

*Portions are based on a standard 8-oz measuring cup.

**EUKANUBA ☙: LAMB & RICE FOR PUPPIES**

**EUKANUBA ADULT MAINTENANCE**

| Dog's Weight (in lbs.) | Cups per Day* |
|---|---|
| 3 - 10 | $^1/_2$ - 1 |
| 10 - 20 | 1 - $1^1/_2$ |
| 20 - 30 | $1^1/_2$ - 2 |
| 30 - 40 | 2 - $2^1/_2$ |
| 40 - 60 | $2^1/_2$ - $3^1/_3$ |
| 60 - 80 | $3^1/_3$ - 4 |
| 80 -100 | 4 - $4^2/_3$ |

*Portions are based on a standard 8-oz measuring cup.

**EUKANUBA ☙: ADULT MAINTENANCE**

**EUKANUBA THE ORIGINAL PREMIUM**

| Dog's Weight (in lbs.) | Moderate Activity | High Activity |
|---|---|---|
| | Cups per Day* | |
| 3 - 10 | $^1/_3$ - $^3/_4$ | $^1/_2$ - 1 |
| 10 - 20 | $^3/_4$ - $1^1/_3$ | 1 - $1^1/_2$ |
| 20 - 30 | $1^1/_3$ - $1^2/_3$ | $1^1/_2$ - 2 |
| 30 - 40 | $1^2/_3$ - 2 | 2 - $2^1/_2$ |
| 40 - 60 | 2 - $2^2/_3$ | $2^1/_2$ - $3^1/_4$ |
| 60 - 80 | $2^2/_3$ - $3^1/_4$ | $3^1/_4$ - 4 |
| 80 -100 | $3^1/_4$ - $3^3/_4$ | 4 - $4^1/_2$ |

*Portions are based on a standard 8-oz measuring cup.

**EUKANUBA ☙: THE ORIGINAL PREMIUM**

# *the ins and outs*
# OF GOOD
# DOG CARE

**You can do regular check-ups yourself.**

All dogs, whether puppy or adult, should get regular check-ups to make sure all is well. You can do a great deal yourself. Once a week or so, take a good look at your dog's eyes, ears and mouth, his coat, toes and nails.

Of course, whenever you're in doubt about your dog's health, visit your veterinarian.

### TIPS TIPS TIPS TIPS TIPS TIPS TI

A dog with an infected eye will rub at it, so if you notice a lot of rubbing going on, take a closer look.

### Coat.
*All dogs need regular grooming. Grooming removes dead hair, dirt and parasites. It stimulates the blood supply to the skin which will result in a healthier and shinier coat. If your dog is long haired or curly haired, you will need to take him to the groomers regularly.*

### Ears.
*In case of excess earwax, you can help to keep his ears healthy by gently cleaning easy-to-reach areas with a moistened cotton-wool ball. Don't probe into his ear with any object. The inner ear is very vulnerable.*

### Eyes.
*Keep his eyes clean by wiping the skin around the inner corners of his eyes gently with a clean cotton-wool ball soaked in warm water.*

### Stools.
*Your dog's stools should be small, firm, with little odor.*

### Paws.
*If something has to be cut out from the fur between or around your dog's paws, use blunt-tipped scissors and be very careful not to cut into the web between his toes.*

### Nails.
*Ask your veterinary surgeon to show you how to clip your dog's nails the first time. Only use dog nail clippers, not scissors. Carefully clip a little at a time to avoid cutting the quick.*

### Mouth.
*It is a good idea to accustom your puppy to having his teeth brushed. Be careful not to hurt his gums, or he'll be too frightened to let you, or the vet, clean his teeth.*

### TIPS TIPS TIPS TIPS TIPS TIPS TIPS TIPS TIPS TIPS TIPS TIPS TIPS TIPS TIPS TIPS TIPS TIPS TIPS TIPS TIP

Bath your dog only when he needs it. Too many baths can strip his coat of oils, making it dull and less waterproof.

Never use human shampoo on your dog. The chemical balance isn't compatible and may dry out his skin.

*training: it pays*

# TO PAY
# ATTENTION

## Training: it pays to pay attention.

You love your dog. You feed him only the best, groom him and show him affection. But if you want him to really thrive, there is still more you must do. We're talking of training and exercise. Training is important for obvious reasons.

You have a responsibility to train your pet to be well-behaved, disciplined member of the community. His psychological health will benef and he will be a much more enjoyable companic if you take the time to train him properly. Exercise is essential for your dog's physical well being.

## Start with a collar and lead.

Get your puppy accustomed to a collar and lead. Start with a narrow, soft collar at first, and let him wear it constantly until he gets used to it. Then attach a light lead to the collar, long enough to reach the ground, and let him drag it around for a few days. Now the trick is to pick up the other end of the lead without starting a tug-of-war. Hold it straight up and walk along, coaxing your puppy to walk along with you. If he lags behind or runs ahead, a few short, gentle tugs are all that should ever be used. Try to stay together, so your pup won't feel the lead too much and won't start to think of it as an uncomfortable restraint.

## Teaching him his name.

The best way to teach your dog his name, is by using it frequently and consistently. Say his name in a bright, animated tone that gets his attention. Do this while playing with him, when you bend down to pet him, or when you're about to put his meal bowl down. He'll soon understand that when you or anyone else says his name, he should pay attention.

## Training and timing.

Your dog is really very conservative. He likes you to put him on a regular schedule in feeding as well as training. Go for short training sessions, starting with five or ten-minute periods, gradually working up to longer sessions Before meals is the best time. A slightly hungry dog is more alert and lively than a just-fed and ready-for-a-nap dog.

## What your dog likes about you?

Your dog is authority minded by nature, so here are a few do's and don'ts for the master.

**Maintain good attitude:** your dog's attitude depends entirely on you, so always end training on a happy note. Both you and your dog will feel pleased.

### A few examples:

Wagging his tail: *"Hello!"*
Tail between his legs, ears down: *"I'm scared."*
Lying on his side, one hind leg in the air: *"You're the boss."*
Licking you: *"Love you, too."*
Forepaws parallel to the ground, head low, tail high:

**Be consistent.** Use the same tone and word every time you give a certain command. If you say, "Come Tasha!" in a bright, encouraging voice during one training session, don't switch to "Here Tasha!" with an authoritative tone during the next. Be firm, and let your dog know training is not play.

**Be patient:** stop when you feel irritable.

**Respond immediately:** your praise or correction should always follow immediately after your dog responds to a command.

**Your tone of voice** is of the utmost importance: praise him extravagantly, correct him with a short, stern "No". Physical reprimands and shouting will never help a dog. A well-trained dog will respond because he wants to please his master, not because he's afraid of him.

**What you may see in your dog.**
As every owner gradually discovers, his dog has a wide sounding range of barks.

From growling to whimpering, from yelping to whining, each has its own distinctive meaning. Listening to your dog, you will soon find out what he's trying to say. But your dog has other ways of expressing himself. A lot of his intentions and feelings can be seen simply from his posture.

*"Let's play!"* Ears high in the air: *"You don't frighten me."*
These are but a few examples. Of course, you'll see a lot more in your own dog.

**Training for competition is lots of fun.**
Two examples of popular sports for dogs clearly demonstrate the fun you and your dog can have with training and competition. Flyball, a relatively new and very fast sport, is a kind of relay race over hurdles. Two teams of dogs, (normally

*How does your own dog express himself? Note some of his particular sounds, postures and facial expressions.*
_____
_____
_____
_____
_____
_____
_____

four per team), race against each other to get the fastest time. The first dog runs over hurdles to a flyball box where he activates a pedal or similar device propelling a ball into the air which he has to catch. He then has to return with it over the same hurdles. Once he has crossed the start/finish line the next dog can set off and repeat the process. The height of the hurdles is decided by the smallest dog, so every team tries to include a small dog.

Agility is another fun sport. Dogs race over a type of obstacle course consisting of various pieces of equipment including a see saw, weaving poles and a flexible tunnel. The course must be completed in order, and each obstacle must also be tackled in a correctly controlled manner. As the name suggests, this sport promotes one of the most valuable basics in your dog.

If you are interested in participating in one of these sports, there are official clubs you can contact who will supply details of regulations and leagues.

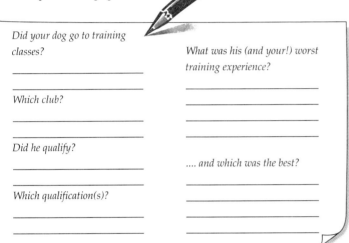

*Did your dog go to training classes?*

_____

*Which club?*

_____

*Did he qualify?*

_____

*Which qualification(s)?*

_____

_____

*What was his (and your!) worst training experience?*

_____

_____

_____

*.... and which was the best?*

_____

_____

_____

Rewards are the greatest help in training. But since all rewards vary greatly in nutritional value, pick healthy ones that don't interfere with your dog's diet. Iams Biscuits may be your best choice.

Take your own dog's natural abilities and limitations into account when starting him on a training schedule.

Do not use your hand to correct your dog, rather use a lightly rolled newspaper. Your hand should always be associated with praise and care.

At 5 to 6 months of age, you may enroll your puppy in an obedience school. It will be useful, and a lot of fun for both of you. If you are interested in showing your dog, contact your local dog club.

*Affix a photo in here.*

*Affix a photo in here.*

**And this is ......**

*Teacher's pet!*

*friends, all*

# KINDS OF FRIENDS

## Fight like cats and dogs.

Cats and dogs aren't always the best of friends.

Your dog may share your house with your cat very happily, but the saying isn't without reason.

An obstacle seems to be the misinterpretation of each other's body language.

The posture your dog uses when he wants to play, unfortunately resembles the pose your cat adopts when she's ready to attack.

It's like saying "How do you do" in a country where these

exact sounds mean "Do you want to fight". In addition, the difference in size may not help either. However, as both have a very keen sense of smell, it seems your cat and dog, will accept each other quite easily when they both have the same "pack smell" - the unique and typical scent of your family, imperceptible to the human nose.

## Young dogs and old dogs.

Usually, a bitch will rule over her puppies, even when they have grown up. But when two dogs from different packs come together, for example a young one and an older one, fighting can result to establish the hierarchical order. This is an inborn instinct, independent of the size of dogs, their sex or their strength. Once the authority clear, there is peace. Try to intervene as little as possible Only when the stronger one gets sick or injured, the power struggle might restart - and the way, fighting does not necessarily imply bloody scenes!

## Your children and your dog.

Anybody who has seen a baby and a puppy playing together will tell you - one way or another, these two understand each other. In general, children and dogs do live together very well - as long as you make sure your children do not harass your dog. For children's development, the company of pets is very important.

*Affix a photo in here.*

**Generation gap? Never heard of it!**

*Affix a photo in here.*

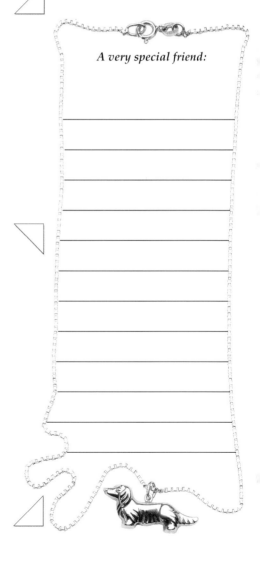

*A very special friend:*

**Friends through thick and thin.**

# TRAVELING TOGETHER

**him used to traveling.**

...ether you live in a town or ...he country, your dog will ...e to get used to traveling. ...he very least, your dog ...uld expect rides to and ...n the veterinarian for ...ck-ups or treatment.

...important for your dog to ...rk up a tolerance for being ...moving vehicle, be it a car, ...or train. Get your dog ...ustomed to rides with a ten- ...ute trip every other day for ...uple of weeks. Gradually ...rease the length of these ...s.

*Affix a photo in here.*

*My first holiday adventure.*

**eck where you are staying - ...ore departure.**

...ou plan to stay in a hotel, ...tel or campsite, check ahead ...nsure that pets are ...lcome.

**...veling Abroad**

...en traveling abroad, remember each country has its own regulations regarding a dog's entrance. Most countries require at least certificates stating good health and proof of recent rabies vaccinations.

But some countries enforce quarantine legislation. Request information before traveling.

TIPS TIPS TIPS TIPS TIPS TIPS TIPS TIPS TIPS TIPS TIPS TIPS TIPS TIPS TIPS

Don't drive your dog immediately after he's eaten, especially if he's prone to car sickness.

Go for a short walk with your dog before departure.

If your dog is used to a certain box, cage or traveling pen, by all means take it with you if it's manageable. Take along his favorite toy or blanket.

When traveling by car, keep it well ventilated. Don't let your dog hang his head out of the window: he could easily get a bug or piece of sharp grit in his eyes or nose.

Stop regularly at a parking area to let your dog out for a drink of water, some exercise, and to relieve himself. Keep him on a lead while he's in a strange place.

Do not leave your dog in the car on hot days. Dogs can suffer from heat stroke very quickly - it can be fatal.

*what's so special about*

# THE IAMS COMPANY

the unique Animal Care
ter - pets are paramount.
Iams Company is no
inary pet food
nufacturer. Ever since its
ndation almost fifty years
, the Company has had a
gle purpose: we want to be
best in creating superior
d for your pet.

establish this superiority,
operate our unique Animal
e Center in Lewisburg,
io, U.S.A. where cats and
gs of many breeds are
erved in a home-like
ironment. A lot of time is
nt playing with the pets
coaching them.

determine their nutritional
ds in different life stages
life styles and we spend
ny animal test days before
accept a new product.

y Eukanuba is the best
can do for your dog.
kanuba is a complete, meat-
ed diet containing a highly
latable formula of animal
teins, animal fats, vitamins,
nerals and carbohydrates.
bags of Eukanuba Dog
ods are formulated with
negaCOAT Nutritional
ence™. OmegaCOAT™
vides an optimal balance
fatty acids to enrich the
ality of your dog's coat
d keep skin cells healthy.
negaCOAT is unmatched
the dog food industry and
supported by university
search. Eukanuba is highly
gestible, so your dog obtains
re usable nutrition from
ery ounce. Benefits? Small,
m stools with little odor
d excellent skin and coat
ndition. You'll see healthy
in and a glossy coat after
out six to eight weeks, and
er several months sound
iscle tone.

Feeding your puppy Eukanuba
from the start, will ensure his
teeth and bones get everything
they need for perfect growth.

**Look at the ingredients and
their balance.**
All Eukanuba dry foods, (apart
from Lamb and Rice which
contains real lamb meat), are
made with chicken and egg,

two of the purest, most
digestible sources of protein.
We insist on nothing less than
the very best ingredients from
the same trusted suppliers,
regardless of raw material
prices or availability. Which is
why every bag of Eukanuba is
always of the same consistent
high quality.

We never use fillers, binders,
artificial colors, flavors, or
preservatives.

## The Eukanuba Range.

Eukanuba is available in bags. There are 5 products in the dry range to fit in with every dog's age and lifestyle.

EUKANUBA PUPPY® SMALL OR LARGE BITES. A complete, balanced high-nutrition food for those all-important first months of growth. Specially formulated to meet the very special needs of a growing puppy. It's an excellent weaning food.

EUKANUBA® ADULT MAINTENANCE. A complete, balanced food providing an excellent maintenance diet for adult dogs with a normal level of activity.

EUKANUBA® THE ORIGINAL PREMIUM. A complete, balanced high-quality food providing optimum nutrition for dogs with normal to high activity levels. It's ideal for pet dogs, show dogs, working dogs and during pregnancy and lactation.

EUKANUBA® LIGHT. A complete, balanced food providing all the nutrients needed by an adult dog if he has a below-average level of activity or a tendency to be overweight.

EUKANUBA® NATURAL™ LAMB & RICE FOR PUPPIES OR FOR DOGS. A complete, balanced quality food for your puppy or dog, prepared with fresh lamb meat. Especially appropriate for puppies or dogs suffering from poor skin or coat conditions.

Eukanuba products are available at pet shops, veterinary clinics, kennels and other specialty pet food outlets.

## Further information.

The Iams Company's sole purpose is enhancing the well-being of cats and dogs through world class quality foods. We are genuinely concerned about your dog's well-being, so if you have any questions about feeding your dog, don't hesitate to contact the pet professionals at 1-800-525-42 or the address below. We'll be pleased to help you.

**The Iams Company**
**Customer Service**
**7250 Poe Avenue**
**Dayton, OH 45414**